Beautiful '

sharing our faith w
and neighbc

a group course

Roger Morgan

ReSource

ReSource – helping to build a church which is diverse, local, renewed in the Spirit and effective in mission

Published by ReSource
13 Sadler Street, Wells, Somerset BA5 2RR
www.resource-arm.net
Charity no. 327035

ISBN 978-1-906363-28-4

Further information and support from ReSource

If you would like support from Roger Morgan or another member of the
ReSource team as you use this course, or if you would like to talk to us about
running outreach events or local missions, please do get in touch by email at
office@resource-arm.net or by phone on 01749 672865.

Additional resources to support your evangelism are available on our website:
Stay Evangelism (the booklet which accompanies this course), *Decision*
(probably the best short introduction to faith for new or potential Christians,
ideal for use with Alpha and outreach events and the *Oikos* prayer cards
(designed to help you to pray for friends who are not yet Christians).

Contents

Beautiful Lives

'May they be won over without a word.. when they see the purity and reverence of your lives. Let your adornment be the inner self with the lasting beauty of a gentle and quiet spirit.' (1 Peter 3.2-4)

'Beauty is commonly trivialized in our culture, whether secular or ecclesial. It is reduced to decoration, equated with the insipidities of "pretty" or "nice." But beauty is not an add-on, not an extra, not a frill. Beauty is fundamental. Beauty is evidence of and witness to the inherent wholeness and goodness of who God is and the way God works. It is life in excess of what we can manage or control.' (Eugene Peterson, *The Jesus Way*, Hodder 2007)

'Beauty of life causes strangers to join our ranks. We do not talk about great things; we live them' (Minucius Felix, Rome, 160-240 AD).

Beautiful Lives

A course to help ordinary Christian believers reach out to their friends and neighbours with the intention that some of these friends and neighbours will become believers too.

Introduction

Beautiful Lives is a group course. The notes contained in this book are for the group leader. Each week of the course involves homework, and this is contained in the separate course member's booklet which should be given to each participant.

Ideally the course leaders will be people who have a clear commitment to evangelism and feel reasonably confident about it. The intention from the beginning is that there will be some new Christians some time soon as a direct result of the course, and the group leaders should be committed to this as an aim.

This course lasts for eight sessions and can be done either weekly or fortnightly (if you feel the group needs to go more slowly, you could divide some of the sessions into two and make the course a bit longer). Each session lasts for 90 minutes. The assumption is that this will fit into a two hour period, giving 30 minutes leeway for coffee, waiting for late arrivals, going home early and so on. The course is written for groups of between four and ten people – larger groups should divide into two.

The course involves the planning and preparation of an event which will take place some time after the course has been completed. This is an event to which course members will invite unchurched friends.

Group leaders are welcome to adapt the notes as they see fit, as long as they cover the same ground as the course in each of the sessions. Those with relatively little experience in evangelism are probably best to follow the notes fairly closely, but more experienced group leaders will want to bring something of their own experience to the sessions and they should feel free to do this.

The homework is designed to encourage and help the group to adopt a lifestyle which is outreaching, deliberately loving, and evangelistic. Each week the group members will enter into their normal lives with the determination to apply what they have learned on the course, and the members will report back to the group at the end of the week. It is essential that each member of the group should enter wholeheartedly into this homework.

The course will only be effective if there is a commitment by the group members to attend all eight sessions. Exceptions can be made to cover particularly difficult personal circumstances, but 100% attendance should be both the aim and the norm. If someone does have to miss a session, another member of the group should meet up with them and help them to catch up. The group members must also be committed to supporting the special outreach event which will follow the course.

Each participant should bring a Bible to the sessions, and the course leader will need a flip chart or whiteboard for some of the sessions. It is assumed that each session will begin with an appropriate welcome, for example with coffee and biscuits being provided as people arrive and greet one another.

Beautiful Lives Week 1

The growth of the Church in Acts

Introduction   (10 mins)

The group leader should ask the members to introduce themselves and then say something about themselves – where they live and with whom, what they do for a living and so on.

Note: The timings are important and need to be carefully watched by the group leader. Here, for example, if you allow 30 minutes for the introduction it will probably spoil the whole session. This is much more likely to be a problem if the group is large.

Evangelism   (10 mins)

Begin with a discussion of the word evangelism – a word which frightens some people. Remind the group that they have come to a course about evangelism and ask them:

- When you hear the word evangelism how do you feel?

Supplementary questions to get the group going might be

- Does the word evangelism make anyone here feel inadequate?
- Does the word evangelism make anyone here feel excited?

Assure the group that the course will make evangelism seem much more possible than it probably does right now.

A choice

The first question for us to think about is "are we
going to go for it?"
Say to the group:

- I want us to imagine that we have a choice.
  We can apply this choice to any group of Christians of which we are members. It might be
  our church, or this group, or any other Christian group to which we
  belong. This is the choice. Imagine that we can choose that five years
  from now the church (or group) will be exactly as it is now, except that
  everyone is five years older. Apart from this we will still be doing much
  the same things with much the same people. Alternatively, we can
  choose that the church will be twice the size that it is now and that
  the new people are all newcomers to faith and have been introduced
  to Christ through our efforts. Which of these options will we choose,
  and why?

Most groups will say that they would rather that their church or group
had doubled in size. Assuming that this is the choice which your group
makes, now ask them what they think it would cost them to achieve this
end. As an example of what it might cost you could say

- If we had twice as many people, this would mean that each of us
  would become responsible for praying for and caring about all these
  new people.

Ask the group what other drawbacks they can see to making the choice
to try to grow.

God's plan

Assuming the group prefers the option of growth, point out that a further
question naturally follows:

- Is the power in our hands – could we grow if we wanted to, or is evangelism too difficult in practice? If we were to try to grow are we likely to succeed or fail?

Explain that to answer this question you are going to begin with some Bible study. The point of this study will be to show that it is, and always has been, God's plan that the Church should grow. It will follow that because this is what God wants, if we co-operate with him and rely on his resources then our evangelism will succeed.

Point out to the group that Christianity began with Jesus and at the beginning there was only Him. Since then the Christian faith has been expanding and expanding – in fact the biggest period of expansion since the time of the early church was the twentieth century.

- Ask the group to turn to **Mark 1.14**. Christianity began when Jesus came into the world and began to preach his message. What, according to Mark 1.14, was his message?

- Now divide the group into pairs and ask each pair to have a look at **John 1.35 – 2.11**. Each pair should answer the question "who were the first people to respond to the message of Jesus, and why did they respond?"

The growth of the Church in the book of Acts (25 mins)

Bring the group together again and ask them to turn to **Acts 1.15**. Say to the group:

- We have seen how it began when Andrew, Peter, Philip and Nathaniel believed in Jesus and gave everything up to follow him. After that the number of disciples grew. Soon there were twelve male disciples and a number of women as well. On one occasion Jesus sent out 70 of his disciples to spread his message. These earliest disciples went through many adventures with Jesus, learning a lot and seeing a lot. Eventually they went through the terrible experience of the crucifixion and then they became the joyful witnesses of the resurrection. By the time we reach Acts 1.15 there were 120 disciples meeting together. So it began with Jesus, and three years later there were 120 Christian disciples. From that beginning the Church has grown and grown until today.

Now tell the group that you are going to look at the early history of growth as it is set out in the book of Acts.

Divide the group into pairs again and ask each pair to work their way through the following verses *(NB this Bible study can be found on the first page of the course member's booklet, so make sure each person has a copy)*.

- Acts 1.8 - Jesus tells his disciples that this will be his last physical appearance to them. Instead the Holy Spirit will come upon them and they will be his witnesses, first in Judea, which was where they were living, then in Samaria, which was the nearest place after that, and then to the world.

- Acts 2.1-4 - The Holy Spirit comes upon the disciples as Jesus had promised.

- Acts 2.22-24 - The disciples actively begin to witness as Jesus had told them to.

- Acts 2.41 - The 120 see 3000 people come to faith in Jesus on a single day.

- Acts 2.42-46 - The new community in Jerusalem, filled by the Holy Spirit.

- Acts 2.47 - Others see this community in action and also become believers.

- Acts 6.7 - The church grows even bigger.

- Acts 11.19-21 - The good news spreads to other cities including Antioch.

- Acts 13.1-5 - Paul and Barnabas are sent out by the church in Antioch to take the gospel to the rest of the world.

Allow about 15 minutes for this Bible study and then bring the pairs back together again. Say to the group: "We saw how, beginning with Jesus, the gospel reached 120 people in three years, and we have now seen how this expanded to include thousands of people in many cities over the next few years." Ask the group how they think Jesus intended this expansion of the Christian faith to end? Then turn together to **Matthew 24.14**. The answer is that evangelism will continue until there are Christian disciples in every part of the world. Then Jesus will return.

This is God's plan and we are part of it. At every stage in the last 2,000 years some Christians have done nothing about evangelism while other Christians have done everything they can to share their faith. Those who have worked at it have always succeeded, because God has always been with them. We ourselves are Christians because of their efforts.

Homework   (10 mins)

Explain that each week there will be homework, and that it will be essential for each person to complete it. Next week you will talk together about how the homework went.

Explain that in this week's homework we learn the first lesson of all effective evangelism, which is that we cannot evangelise people unless we first learn to love people. To teach this lesson Jesus told the story of the Good Samaritan. Ask the group to turn to **Luke 10.25-37** and invite someone to read the passage.

Ask the group to say what the difference was between the Samaritan (v 33) and the other two men (v 31-32). The answer is that the Samaritan was moved with pity - he really cared what was happening to the man who was hurt. The other two men seem not to have cared.

This week the homework challenges us to spend our days doing our best to live like the Good Samaritan. The homework notes suggest that to achieve this we must first learn to go through life slowly. Many people today are always in a hurry and are preoccupied with themselves and their own business, and as a result never notice what is going on around them. Our task this week will be to go through life slowly enough to take in the people whom God has brought to us to share our world. During the week we will try to notice people - our families, our work colleagues, our neighbours, even the people we pass in the streets. Whenever we have the opportunity we will do what we can to help them.

Prayer   (10 mins)

Turn to **Acts 1.8** and remind the group of the historical context of this verse. Jesus is making his last appearance to his disciples. He is telling them what is going to happen next: they will go into the world and represent him as his witnesses. To help them to do this he will give them the gift of the Holy Spirit.

Ask the group to stand, form a circle and hold hands. Say to the group

- I would like the group to take the homework really seriously as we do this course. This week we are being sent out into the world to really love people. To do this we, like the earliest disciples, will need the Holy Spirit to warm up our hearts.

Ask each person to pray for the person on their left and the person on their right and earnestly ask that the Holy Spirit will come upon them and equip them for the task. This prayer can be made in silence but if you feel the group is up for it then ask everyone to pray out loud at the same time.

Beautiful Lives Week 2

Go evangelism and Stay evangelism

Homework review   (20 mins)

Begin by giving everybody an opportunity to talk about the homework.
How did the week go? Did they manage to go through life more slowly?
Did anything happen as a result? Have there been any opportunities for
conversations with people? Have there been opportunities to help
people in any way?

If the group has been taking things seriously then each person should
have stories to tell. So allow plenty of time. If the group is a big one then
it will save time if you do this exercise in two or more separate groups.

Go Evangelism and Stay Evangelism   (15 mins)

Ask everyone to look at **Matthew 28.18-20** and explain
that these words were spoken by Jesus after he was
raised from death. Jesus tells his disciples to go: they
are to go to new places and take the gospel to new
people. Eventually the call to follow Jesus will be taken
to every nation on earth.

Now look together at **Luke 8.38-39**. This man, now in his right mind, was
keen to be one of those whom Jesus would ask to leave his home and go
to other places. But Jesus tells him to stay where he is and talk to the
people he already knows.

Explain that in this course we will use the term "go evangelism" when
Jesus calls someone to leave their home and go to another place in
order to evangelise the people there. And we will use the term "stay

evangelism" when Jesus does not call a person to go anywhere but rather asks them to stay and witness to the people at home.

Ask the group to think

- Who is the person who most influenced you to become a Christian?"

- What was it about this person that first attracted you? What was special about them?

Allow everyone to answer and then ask the question

- Did this crucial person come to you from another place or was it someone from your home territory?

In other words you are asking the group whether they came to know Christ through go evangelism or stay evangelism.

Let each person answer, and then summarise by saying something like "It looks as if 7 of us were won by stay evangelism and 3 of us by go evangelism" (or whatever the numbers are). Your group may be an exception, but you will find that in nearly all groups far more people have come to faith through stay evangelism than through go evangelism. From the beginning this has always been the case, and it remains the case today.

Explain that this course is aimed at training us to be stay evangelists. Stay evangelism is the method of evangelism that God uses the most.

In Stay Evangelism actions speak louder than words (15 mins)

Put the group into pairs and ask each pair to look at both **Colossians 1.3-7** and **1 Peter 3.1-2**. For each passage they should try to answer three questions:

1. Who are the evangelists?

2. Are they stay evangelists or go evangelists?
3. What methods did the evangelists use?

Bring the group together again and allow time for them to share their answers.

In the first case Epaphras was the evangelist; he was a go evangelist who went to Colossae to bring the message of the gospel. The Colossians were won by his words, which were anointed by the Holy Spirit.

In the second passage the wives were the evangelists; they were stay evangelists who won their husbands entirely by the way they behaved, without using any words at all. It was their *behaviour* that spoke and which was anointed by the Holy Spirit - just as effectively as Epaphras's words had been.

Remind the group of what they said a moment ago about the people who influenced them. Again there can be exceptions but most people will have shared that what impacted them was something about the way these people lived – what **1 Peter 3.2** describes as 'the beauty and reverence of their lives'. It is beautiful lives that win others. This is the challenge of stay

evangelism – to learn how to live a beautiful life in the power of the Holy Spirit. This is why we have called this course *Beautiful Lives*.

The Holy Spirit   (15 mins)

Turn again to **Acts 1.8**, which you looked at last week. You saw then that those who were appointed to witness to Jesus need the gift of the Holy Spirit on their lives. Those who try to do evangelism - whether go evangelism or stay evangelism - in their own strength will fail.

Explain that in a moment we will pray for the gift of the Holy Spirit as we did last week, but that before we do that we will look together at **Galatians 5.22-23**. Ask the group:

- What kind of people will we become if the Holy Spirit comes upon our lives?

- Is it possible to live like this by ourselves, that is without the help of the Holy Spirit?

- Can you can think of someone you know who does live like this – someone who exhibits love, joy, peace, patience, kindness, goodness, faithfulness, gentleness and self control?

Put people into pairs again and ask each pair to look at the following verses:

- Acts 2.38
- John 7.39
- Luke 11.13

Ask each pair to answer the question "To what kind of person is the Holy Spirit given?"

Bring the group together again and invite them to share their answers.

Then summarise: if we turn from other things (repentance) and put our trust and our hope in Jesus (belief), and when we have done that we ask for the Holy Spirit to be given to us, then the Holy Spirit will come and fill our lives. Then our lives too will change. Love, and joy, and peace, and all the fruits of the Spirit will grow within our hearts and become evident in our lives.

Praying for the Holy Spirit   (15 mins)

You will find a copy of this prayer in the course
member's book:

"Lord Jesus, thank you for the gift of life you have given
me. From today I commit myself to making a new start.
I am sometimes tempted to trust in myself or in other
things, but I promise that from today I will try to trust
you for all the big issues in my life. I know I have not
always lived as I should, and sometimes I get my
priorities all wrong. I want to become the person you made me to be. I want to
turn away from anything that is wrong, and today I promise to try to make you
the most important thing in my life.

I commit myself today to love and serve you by giving time to developing my
relationship with you, and by the way I live among other people. Please Lord fill
me with your Holy Spirit, so that I may display your presence by the way that I
live. May your love flow from me to every person I meet. May my heart shine
because it is filled with your joy and your peace. May I be gentle, patient, kind
and good. May I learn faithfulness, reliability and self-control, so that my choices
are Christ-like. In Jesus' name, Amen."

Explain that this is a prayer which we should say every day, and that we
are going to say it together now. Ask each person to take a moment to
read through the prayer, so that they can be sure that when they say it
they will be saying it sincerely because they really mean it.

Give the group a few moments to reflect. When people are ready, invite
them to stand and say the prayer aloud together.

When you have finished ask the group if they will please join hands and
ask each person in turn to pray for the person on their left. Begin yourself
as the leader, and continue round the circle until someone prays for you.
When you pray you should simply ask that the Holy Spirit will be given to
the person you are praying for.

Homework

Finally ask everyone to turn to page 9 in the
member's coursebook, and put them into pairs
to together at the homework notes for this week.

After five minutes interrupt the pairs to say that
they will have seen that it will be very important
to find a regular time and place to pray each day.
Ask them to decide now what that time and place
will be and share that with their partner.

Beautiful Lives Week 3

Who are our friends and neighbours?

Introduction and homework review   (25 mins)

As last week allow time for each person to share.
Did this week go better than the previous week?
Was it different? Did they remember to seek
refreshment from the Lord? Did they establish a
pattern of daily prayer? Was there evidence of
the Holy Spirit working in their lives? Allow each
person to tell one or two stories.

Listing the people we know   (10 mins)

Explain that this week we are going to think about the
people our lives are reaching. Give each person a
piece of paper and ask them to make a list of all the
people they know who are not churchgoers. They
should not include people from the past who now live
100 miles away; make it clear that you would like
them to include only people they sometimes see in
the course of their normal daily lives. Examples of
people they could include would be:

- family members who do not go to church and who live nearby
- people who live in the same street even if they cannot remember their
  names
- work colleagues
- people they meet through their children or grandchildren
- shopkeepers, doctors, dentists, in fact anyone who serves them in any
  way
- anyone they have fun with or relax with.

18

Almost anybody can make a list of 20 people whom they know. Most people can reach 50 and some many more.

Allow enough time for this exercise to be done thoroughly.

People we know well

(20 mins)

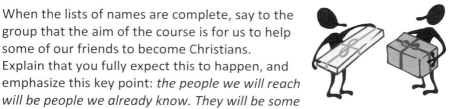

When the lists of names are complete, say to the group that the aim of the course is for us to help some of our friends to become Christians. Explain that you fully expect this to happen, and emphasize this key point: *the people we will reach will be people we already know. They will be some of those whose names we have just written down.* These people are given to us by God ,and they are our responsibility and not anyone else's. It is our job to reach them with the love of God if we possibly can.

Now make the point that we are much more likely to reach the people we have listed if we first get to know them quite well. The better we know people, the more interested they become in us and in what makes us tick. People we know well are much more likely to ask questions.

On the whole people feel they know us better once they have set foot in the place where we live. So ask the group to put a tick against each person on their list who has ever been inside their home.

One of the best ways to get to know people is by having fun with them. Ask the group to put a tick against a name if they have ever had any fun with that person. So at this stage each person on their list will have either two ticks, one tick or no ticks beside their name.

Remind the group of the story of the Good Samaritan. Sometimes we get an opportunity to do something for another person; whenever we help someone it says something about us, especially if we had to go out of our way to do so. So ask them now to put a tick against any person on their list whom they have ever been able to help – in whatever way. Looking again at the lists, some people will now have three ticks beside their name, but some will have none at all.

Now point out that it is possible to know a lot about someone without ever really sharing your heart with them or they with you. So ask the group to put a tick against all the people with whom they have ever shared a heart-to-heart conversation. Don't make this too difficult – a ten minute conversation about something that bothers someone counts as a heart-to-heart. Whenever that happens the relationship moves on a long way.

Look together at **Matthew 5.16** – it is the way we live that brings glory to God. Last week we saw that the key to stay evangelism is leading a beautiful life. Ask the group to add a tick if they think a person on their list has ever seen them at their best. Examples might be:

- coping with difficulties
- being patient with a difficult person
- being kind to strangers
- going the second mile for someone

Has that person seen you being loving, joyful, at peace, patient, kind, good, gentle, faithful and self controlled?

Look together at **1 Peter 3.15**. In stay evangelism we do not witness aggressively. What we do is live as well as we can and serve others as best we can, and wait for them to ask us questions. When they do, we need to be ready. Ask the group to add a tick if they have ever had a conversation in which someone has asked them about themselves and this has led to a conversation about their faith, or about God, or about church.

This makes a maximum of six ticks. The seventh is rather surprising. Ask the group to add a tick if they have known this person for less than three years. The reason is that the longer you know someone the harder it becomes to raise the subject of God or faith. Indeed if we know someone for a very long time and the subject has never come up, the best policy is to pick our moment and then be very direct about it. (But these are exceptional cases).

Making a prayer list   (10 mins)

Ask each person in the group to now make a shorter list. On this list should go first of all the names of all the people to whom they have given five or more ticks. These are people whom they already know quite well. In addition ask them to add the names of other people who have fewer than five ticks but whom they feel motivated to get to know better.

Explain that if they add a name then they are making a commitment to do something to get to know that person better. This will be part of the homework for the coming week. Each person should add at least two names from those on their list who have fewer than five ticks. They can add more if they like, but not too many because in writing the name they are making a commitment to do something about it soon.

Allow the group to think and pray about who these extra people should be, and then collect together these short lists and promise to print out a complete list of names by next week. You will probably find that you now have about five names for each person in the group, maybe more. Explain that later you will be using this list of names for your prayers together.

Praying for these people   (20 mins)

Ask the group to be quiet now, to close their eyes and to think about all the things they have because they are Christians which non Christians do not have. After a few minutes get a flip chart or a board or just a piece of paper which you put on the floor. Write on the top: "The good things that Jesus brings

into our lives" and then as the group comes up with the answers write down everything they say. So on the flip chart it will say something like

- the Holy Spirit
- inner peace
- inner joy
- answers to prayer
- the promises of God
- the hope of heaven

When you have finished the list, ask the group to close their eyes and imagine each of the people on their shortlist standing in front of them. Ask them then to imagine their friend changing so that he or she has each of the things which we have just listed; and to pray for them that this will happen.

Homework   (5 mins)

Finally ask everyone to turn to page 13 in the member's coursebook, and put them into pairs to together at the homework notes for this week.

Beautiful Lives Week 4

Telling our story

The core list of people we long to see become Christians
(25 mins)

Hand out copies of a printed list of the names which you gathered from last week's session. To recap, remember that we expected about five names for each person in the group; some of these are people who received five or more ticks in the exercise last week, and some are people we know less well but are committed to try and get to know better.

Put the group into pairs to talk about the people on their lists and to pray for them. After about ten minutes call the group together and ask them how they got on with the business of making contact with the two or more people whom they added to the list last week. Give them the chance to tell any stories about anything that happened last week or anything they learned from their prayer times.

Paul's story
(10 mins)

Turn to **Acts 26.1-23** and read the passage as a group. This is Paul telling the story of his own spiritual journey to a King who was called Agrippa. Ask the group

- If you had been Agrippa what effect would this story have had on you?

Look again at verse 1. Paul told his story because Agrippa gave him the opportunity; probably Paul told his story at every opportunity. Paul was a go evangelist, and go evangelists do get many opportunities to tell their story. Stay evangelists get fewer chances - but we have to learn to take them when they come. Ask the group

- When do you think that opportunities will come for us to tell our story?

Look together at **1 Peter 3.15**. Ask the group:

- When does Peter say we should tell our story?

The answer is that we should tell our story whenever we are asked. Remind the group that stay evangelism is never aggressive – we wait to be asked, and we must then be ready. So ask them:

- Why would anyone ask us about our faith?

The answer is that they will only ask us when they see that there is something special about the way that we live. Then curiosity will take over - especially when there is an inner need in the person. Ask if anyone in the group has had any conversations about their faith since the course began?

Telling each other   (10 mins)

The main purpose of today's session is to help us to prepare to write down our own stories, so that if anyone asks us we are ready, as Paul was ready.

A common form of question that people ask is "Have you always gone to church?" or "Have you always been a Christian?" Explain that the way to answer these questions is not to simply say yes or no but to respond by telling the story of how you came to believe in Jesus and what difference this has made.

Put the group back into pairs and ask them to share their stories with each other.

24

Two kinds of Christian   (5 mins)

Explain to the group that for purposes of story telling there are two kinds
of Christian. Explain the two kinds to the group:

1. The first kind are like Paul; like Paul you were not
   brought up in a Christian home, or if you were
   your parents' faith failed to capture your heart
   until much later.

2. The second kind are like Timothy (see 2 Timothy
   1.3 --5). Your faith was learned from your family
   and was embraced from the beginning and never
   abandoned.

Ask the group members to say which of these two kinds of Christian each
of them is - are they more like Paul or more like Timothy?

Writing down our stories   (25 mins)

It's time now to begin to think out our stories. Ask those who are more
like Paul to prepare their story in three parts (you may want to hand out
some pre-prepared sample testimonies to help them):

1. A description of your life before conversion
   (as Paul did in Acts 26.2-11)

2. The detailed story of your conversion
   (see Acts 26.12-18)

3. A description of your life since conversion
   (see Acts 26.19-23)

Before they begin, invite them to notice how Paul's story is made more
effective by the contrast between part 1 and part 3; this contrast
illustrates the transformation that was brought about by his conversion.
In part 1 Paul describes himself as a persecutor of the Christian faith; in
part 3 Paul describes himself as an advocate of the Christian faith.

Persecutor to advocate is obviously a massive change! Say to those who are more like Paul that you would like them to think what the transformation was in their own case. For example some people live very bad lives before conversion and very good lives afterwards (St Augustine is a well known example). And some people were very unhappy before conversion and afterwards full of joy. Ask each person not to try and fit themselves into one of these types but to honestly think it out – in what way or ways has Jesus changed their life?

Tell this group who are more like Paul that you want them to spend ten minutes thinking this out. You do not want them to write out their stories at this stage (that will be the homework), but to work out in their minds first the contrast between part 1 and part 3 and then what the content of the three sections needs to be if they are to convey to someone else what becoming a Christian has meant to them.

Then say to those who are more like Timothy that you also want them to think out their story in three parts (again you may want to offer some examples). This time the parts are:

1. Childhood memories of faith

2. The story of your calling to serve the Lord (see 2 Timothy 1.6)

3. Adult outworkings of this calling

For this group the most difficult part may be the middle one. Tell them that the way to write this is to first make a list of the key principles which are driving their life now, and then a list of the key purposes which are filling their hearts and minds. Once this is done they should think out what happened in their relationship with God which has led them to these principles and purposes. Did God speak? Did God challenge them? What exactly happened? It is that story which will constitute part 2.

Now give everyone ten minutes to spend on their own thinking through how they would tell their story. They may make some notes if they like, but at this stage there is no need to write anything.

More practice at telling each other (10 mins)

Finally put people into pairs (but not with the same person as before) and ask each person to share their story with the other, keeping to the outlines above.

Explain that the homework this week asks us to write out our stories, allowing 100 words for each part. (Note - if people are not used to writing, you may wish to suggest they use simple bullet points and work the testimony out in their heads).

Conversations (5mins)

Explain that you want to point out one thing that will come up in the homework this week and next:

- From time to time you will find, during a conversation with a non Christian friend, that your friend starts to ask you about yourself. This is when you may be able to tell your story.

This always happens during a conversation. If we never get into conversations with people, then sharing our stories will never happen. So in week 6 of the course there will be some training on how to conduct a conversation.

Explain to the group that you would like them, as part of the homework, to plan ahead two weeks and to set up some conversations either on a one to one basis or a couple to couple basis. They may like to invite a friend or friends round for a meal, or arrange to go out somewhere with someone, or to fix up a lunch appointment. This will usually need to be planned ahead - which is why it is part of the homework for this week.

Beautiful Lives Week 5

How we live

The Holy Spirit

(5 mins)

When you have welcomed people to the meeting, turn to **Matthew 5.16** and ask the group:

- What, according to Jesus, will lead other people to give glory to God?

The answer is the way that we live. Remind the group of the theme of the course which is *Beautiful Lives*. The idea is that we will try to live such beautiful lives that those who see the way we live will be attracted to us and also attracted to our God.

Turn to **Galatians 5.22-23**, which describes some of the qualities of the beautiful life. These qualities flow from the presence of the Holy Spirit in our lives, and we have seen that a key to living this way is to ask each day to be filled by the Spirit. We have been using a prayer which is printed in the course member's book, week 2. Ask the group to turn to this prayer. Say it together as a group.

Telling our stories

(30 mins)

Remind the group that last week's homework was to write out our stories and then share them with two friends and invite their comments. Ask the group how this went.

Now put the group into threes and ask them to share their stories with each other. After each person has finished the others should encourage them and offer any constructive comments.

Wholeheartedness

We have been using the story of the Good Samaritan to inspire us to live beautiful lives. We have been trying to go through life more slowly and to notice what is going on for the people we meet. Encourage the group to please keep this up.

Explain that today we will look at two other aspects of living beautifully for God. The first of these is wholeheartedness.

Turn to **Colossians 3.23**. Explain that this verse was written by St Paul specifically to Christians who were slaves. How could Paul advise these people, who had very little free time and no choice about where they lived and what they did all day, about the best way to serve Jesus? Point out that Paul's answer is that they could serve Jesus best by the attitude that they had to their work. Paul is asking them to be wholehearted about everything that they do.

Ask each person to tell the group what activity or activities occupy most of their time. Who (that is, which other people) observes how they go about those activities?

When everyone has shared say that the key question is

- If these people see the way that we do things, what will they think about us? Do they see a beautiful life in which everything is done as well as possible, or do they see a sloppy, careless, half-hearted life?

Ideally, Paul says they should be seeing someone who is consumed with a desire to please God by the way that they do everything. We are not to work half-heartedly but with a determination to be the best that we can be.

A group exercise

As an exercise prepare a task for each person in
the group to do now. One possibility would be to
bring some shoe cleaning materials and ask each
person to clean and polish their own shoes, or you
could together clean the house in which you are
meeting. Or everyone could sit down and write a
letter to someone who needs a letter. The point of
the exercise is that everyone should do whatever
they do to the utmost, not worrying about what
the others are thinking but only about what God is thinking. When you
have finished share with each other how you felt about this task.

Integrity

People love to say of Christians that they are
hypocrites, and indeed the problem is that in some
cases this may be true! A stay evangelist cannot
afford to be a hypocrite; hypocrisy destroys the
power of our witness.

Ask the group to turn to the course member's book
and look at this list of questions:

1. Are you able to forgive others no matter how they have hurt you?

2. Are you able to promote others and not yourself?

3. Are you able to aim for peace with all people?

4. Are you always honest?

5. Are you able to keep your temper?

6. Is your speech honouring of others or are you critical of them
   when they are absent?

7. Are you being faithful in your marriage in both your actions and
   your thoughts?

8. Do you always remain sober?

9.   Do you live simply or extravagantly?

10. Are you free from anxiety or do you worry a lot?

11. Do you always keep your word?

12. Are you always on time for appointments?

13. Do you meet disappointment or misfortune with faith and cheerfulness?

Say to the group that people judge us all the time by whether or not we do these things. Most would say that this is the right way to live. But although people do not manage to live this way themselves, they do expect us to! People who know us well know whether we do or whether we don't.

Take the first item on the list and ask the group

- If we fail to forgive when someone has wronged us, how will this weaken our witness?

Ask the same question for some of the other items.

Ask each member of the group to choose one of these areas in which they would most like to grow. Put the group into threes to share and pray for each other. Each person should begin by confessing the area they have chosen and asking for God's help; the others will then pray for them.

Homework   (5 mins)

Before you go home give the group some time to have a brief look at the homework for this week (this can be found on p.20 of the member's course-book). In particular remind them of the challenge to set up conversations with non-Christian friends, not for the coming week but for the week after.

Beautiful Lives Week 6

Getting into conversation

Reporting back   (10 mins)

Welcome people to the meeting. This week use the report back time to talk about prayer. Ask people to get into threes, and invite them to tell one another how their daily prayer times are working out. Have they managed to establish a pattern of daily prayer? What difference has this made to them?

Sharing plans   (10 mins)

The homework for Week 5 asked people to plan ahead so that this week they would have some opportunities for one-on-one conversations with non Christians (or perhaps couple to couple). Keeping to the same threes, ask people to share what they have planned. If any have forgotten to do this, perhaps they could use this time now to make some plans.

Ideas on how to hold a conversation   (25 mins in total)

1. Facts   (7 mins)

Most of the rest of this session will be about how to conduct those conversations. Tell the group that today we will practise on each other, and then during the week we will do things for real.

Begin by putting the group members into pairs. If there is an odd number, leave yourself out. It is important for the success of this exercise to get the pairing right - so choose who goes with whom yourself. The key thing is that people who know each other well should not be paired together.

Once people are in pairs, ask them to number off so that one of each pair is designated as number one and the other as number two. Once this has been done say that you are going to give instructions to the number twos about how to conduct a conversation with their number one. This is not a role play - the idea is that they should just be themselves.

Ask the number twos to begin the conversation by asking a question which is pitched at the factual level, for example "Where were you brought up?" or "Where did you go to school?" or "What have you been doing today?" The question can be anything which expresses interest in the other person without being too intrusive.

Before they start, explain that as the number ones share facts about themselves, the number twos should be looking for ways to make connections with them. So the conversation might go something like:

- What have you been doing today?
- I had a day off today, so I did some shopping in Shrewsbury ...

The number two then makes a connection:

- Oh that's funny, I was shopping in Shrewsbury today too – where did you go?

Ask the number twos to get started and allow the conversation to go on for just four minutes. Then interrupt.

2. Opinions   (7 mins)

Explain to the group that it is very interesting and not at all threatening to conduct a conversation entirely at the factual level - but that if we are to get close to someone we will need to move on from this level.

Stage 1 in a conversation is sharing facts and making connections; stage 2 is holding a discussion. It will now be up to the number twos to switch the conversation away from fact sharing and turn it into a discussion. Explain to the group that the way this is done is to ask the person you are talking to for his or her opinion about something. So if you have been talking about shopping in Shrewsbury you could ask "Do you like Shrewsbury?" or "What do you think about the new development?" – anything that follows naturally from the previous factual conversation.

Make sure the group understands this, and then invite the number twos to carry on the conversation from where you interrupted them. As they talk, ask them to be thinking how they might develop the conversation into a discussion. Once the number one has given his or her opinion about something the number two should respond - saying for example that they couldn't agree more, or that they see where the person is coming from but the way they look at it is like this.

If the number twos find that they disagree with the opinion expressed by their number one they should not be afraid to express that disagreement as long as it is done in a way that shows respect.

Get them started and again interrupt after four minutes.

3. Feelings (7 mins)

Now explain that Stage 3 of a good conversation is sharing feelings. If we know someone well then we can reach this level very quickly, but if we do not know them well it is very intrusive to go straight to the feelings level.

Explain that what you would like the number twos to do now is to move the conversation on from opinions and try to reach the feelings stage. So you would like them to carry on the conversation from the point at which you interrupted them. As they talk they should now be asking themselves what it might feel like to be this other person. Perhaps they have learned that this person is 45 and single – what might that feel like? Perhaps they have learned that this person has moved to the area very recently – what might that feel like? As soon as the number two has decided the best area to explore they should ask a feeling question. For example "Before you moved to Shrewsbury you were in Ipswich a long time and must have lots of friends there – do you find that you miss your friends?" But do not be too intrusive. "It must be tough being single at your age" is not a good question for the early stages of a relationship!

Explain that when the number one shares their feelings, it is very important for the number two to respond well. For example

- You should never say "I know how you feel" - you probably don't.

- You should never turn a feelings statement back into a discussion. So for example if your friend has told you how hard it has been to move from Ipswich to Shrewsbury, it is not good to respond by saying "In my opinion change is good for you".

The vital thing is that the person is made to feel that you are listening, that you are trying to understand, and that you are able to stand on their ground and feel with them.

Tell the number twos to carry on the conversation from where they left off and to try to reach the feelings level. Interrupt again after four minutes.

4. Continuing the relationship   (4 mins)

Now ask the number twos

- You have been talking to your number one for about 12 minutes now. Who feels they are a bit closer now than they were 12 minutes ago?"

You will find that almost everyone has enjoyed this exercise.

Suggest to the number twos that although the conversation has to end now, as all conversations do, it's a good idea before you break up to make a suggestion to the other person for how the relationship may be continued. For example they could suggest that it would be nice to meet up again sometime; or offer to lend them a book, or to help them in some way.

Give the number twos 3 minutes to suggest something to their number ones.

Telling your story   (5 mins)

Summarise by saying something like this. "What is happening in these conversations is that you are taking an interest in the other person. Sometimes you will find that the person reciprocates by taking an interest in you - just as you want to get to know them, so they are equally keen to make connections with you, to discuss things  with you, and to learn how you feel about life. If someone asks you about yourself, then feel free to tell them. This is when the story of your journey with God may come in – not in every conversation, but you will be surprised how often it does."

Reversing Roles   (20 mins)

Now it's time for the number ones to practise on the number twos - but before they do, ask them to change partners. This time tell them that you will not interrupt but that you want them to follow the same pattern, beginning with facts and trying to make connections; then moving on to a discussion by asking for opinions; then wondering what must it feel like to be this person and moving the conversation onto feelings. And then they should end by making some suggestion for how the relationship might be continued.

Bringing our friends into contact with our group (20 mins)

Remind the group that in Week 4 you gave them an
up to date list of about 50 friends, people who we
know well, or hope to know well.

Perhaps it is some of these people whom group
members plan to have conversations with in the
week ahead.

Now is the time to start thinking about how to put on an event to which
the group can invite these 50 friends. Explain that this event will be held
in a few weeks' time, after the course is over. Now is the time to begin to
think about this event. You will continue to plan for it over the last two
weeks of the course.

Say to the group that on the whole people will come to events if they feel
they will fit in. Refer the group members to the following list which they
will find in the course member's book:

Would your particular friends feel comfortable if

1. They knew they were coming to a discussion?
2. They knew they were coming to enjoy a good meal?
3. They were coming to share in some kind of outing?
4. They knew that they would be listening to a good speaker?
5. They knew that they would be playing a game of some sort?
6. They knew that they would be listening to people telling their stories?
7. They knew that if they wanted to someone would pray for them in
   confidence?
8. They knew that there would be background music?
9. They knew that there would be singing of religious songs?

Ask each member of the group to go through the list and write 'yes' or
'no' or 'maybe' beside each one. As they do this remind them that it is

not whether we feel comfortable that counts but whether our friends would feel comfortable.

Then collect in the results. This exercise will help you to design the coming event.

Now explain to the group that whether or not the event has a formal speaker it does need to have a topic, so that people know what they are coming to and so that they will go away with something really helpful to chew over. The following topics are listed in the course member's book. Ask the group to say which they think their unchurched friends would most like to come to (point out that this may be different from the ones they themselves are most interested in):

1. Stress – causes, symptoms and cures, and where faith fits in

2. Money, sex and power – good for us or bad for us?

3. How to be happy

4. Has Science made God unnecessary?

5. When things go wrong—strategies for coping in life's most difficult moments

6. How to deal with difficult people

7. How to live a life that makes a difference

8. How to make relationships work

9. Secrets of family life

10. How to find a faith which works

A simple way to decide which topic would be the best to invite people to is to give each person present three votes and ask them to vote for three topics. The topics with the most votes are likely to be those which would command the most interest.

Explain to the group that you will take away what they have said and come back next week with a proposal for an event to which we will invite our friends. But ask now if anyone has any ideas.

End by praying together that you will come up with a helpful event, and for those you will invite to it.

Pray also for the conversations that you have planned for the coming week.

Beautiful Lives Week 7

Speaking and loving

Returning to our core list
(5 mins)

Welcome people to the group. Start by returning to the list of the 50 or so names that you collected together in week 3 and handed out in week 4. Ask if there are any extra names that people wish to add and make a note so that you can update your master list.

Explain to the group that our aim now will be to do everything we can to enable these particular people to come to know Jesus just as we do. If we fail we will not abandon our relationship with these people – they still matter to us and they probably always will, but we shall know that we have at least tried. The purpose of today's session is for us to see how God wants us to go about it.

The parable of the sower
(15 mins)

Turn to **Mark 4.1-20** and ask someone to read it out loud. Then ask:

- If we were to make every effort to reach these 50 people with the message of Jesus what would happen?

The group may get the point or it may be that you will have to explain the parable - but it is very important that everyone understands and believes what Jesus taught. This parable is crucial to an understanding of all evangelism. The explanation of the parable is as follows:

Each of our 50 friends will make one of are 4 possible responses; we will almost certainly experience all four of them.

1. There will be those among the 50 who will be untouched by anything we say or do. They may even be hostile. There is nothing at all that we can do about this. The important point is not to allow these people to discourage us. Stay evangelism, like all evangelism, is sometimes very difficult.

2. There will be those who appear to be very positive but it will all come to nothing. These people are the ones among our 50 who are people pleasers, who try to please whoever they are with. While they are with us they will seem enthusiastic about what we say, but when they are away from us they will try to please others. That is why they seem to blow hot and cold. Stay evangelism, like all evangelism, can be very disappointing.

3. There will be those who we can welcome into our churches, but the sad truth is that we will never really reach their hearts. These people believe in Jesus in their heads but will never make him pre-eminent in their lives. Some of them care too much for the riches and pleasures of this life to ever focus fully on the next. Others are full of anxiety; their hearts are preoccupied by worries of one kind or another and they cannot bring themselves fully to trust in Jesus.

4. There will be some among the 50 who will become wholehearted believers in Jesus; these people will in time influence many more. Jesus is teaching us through the parable not to be put off by the disappointment of the first three groups but to carry on diligently searching for those whose hearts are like good soil.

The Word of God

Now ask the group to look at the passage again and tell you by what means they think we might reach the hearts of this fourth group.

The answer is by the Word of God. Explain that our task as evangelists is to deliver the Word of God to these 50 people. The parable promises us that if we do this, some of them will hear the Word of God, believe it, give their hearts to Jesus, and become fruitful.

So the next question is

- What is the Word of God?

Ask the group and see what they think. Some people will say that the Word of God is the Bible. This is not so far from the truth but it is not quite right. The Bible is often the way that the Word of God is communicated, but it is not the only way. The Word of God is exactly what it says it is – the Word of God is God speaking.

As a group look at **Isaiah 55.11**.

Explain that when God speaks, something always happens. When we speak – for example if we give an instruction – we know from experience that often nothing happens. But when God speaks, things do happen.

As a group look at **Genesis 1.3**. When God spoke what happened?

Finally look at **John 1.1-5** where John teaches that Jesus is the Word of God. Jesus is the most powerful way in which God has ever spoken his Word. Jesus, the living Word, accomplished the purpose for which he was sent. He communicated God's Word by everything he was, by the way he lived, by the words he spoke and by his prayers. Jesus always had an impact and God's purpose was accomplished in every personal encounter Jesus made. The parable of the sower shows how people sometimes responded positively and sometimes negatively to the Word he spoke to them.

Our task today as stay evangelists is to be like Jesus in today's world. We can only do this as we are inhabited by the same Holy Spirit who inhabited Jesus. Then our lives, our words and our prayers will be the Word of God and they will always have a powerful impact. It is certainly true that the Bible is the Word of God, but it essential for us to grasp that filled with the Holy Spirit we ourselves are also the Word of God.

Our love for each other   (15 mins)

Ask the group

- What have we learned so far about how we go about being the Word of God to our friends and neighbours?

Let the group answer but summarise as follows:

1. We become the Word of God when we are filled with the Holy Spirit

2. We become the Word of God when we love our neighbours as ourselves

3. We become the Word of God by being wholehearted in everything we do

4. We become the Word of God when we live by our principles and not as hypocrites

5. We become the Word of God by telling our story, the way that the Word of God has spoken into our own lives.

Then say that there is one other thing to say about being the Word of God which is probably more important than any of the others. Ask the group to turn to **John 13.34-35**, and say that the most important way in which we communicate the Word of God is given in these verses. Ask them what this way is? Many people will look at the verses and give the answer that we

communicate God's Word to people by our love for them. But this is not what these verses actually say, and it's extremely important that the group grasps this. So ask them to look again at the verses.

These verses in John 13 teach that we communicate the Word of God not by our love for other people but by our love for each other. It is as people see our community and how it works that God will speak to them more powerfully than he does in any other way. It is true that as individual Christians we communicate God's Word by everything we are or do, and this is a big part of stay evangelism. But even more important is the impact of our corporate life. If God is in the midst of us, then as people see us then they will get a glimpse of God - and sometimes much more than a glimpse.

Help the group to see that follows from this that the 50 non Christian friends we are trying to reach, who we trust are already being spoken to through our individual lives, must at some point be brought into our community so that they can see what real Christianity is like. That is why we are going to hold an event to which we can invite them all.

A group of Christians filled by the Holy Spirit   (15 mins)

The big question is this: when we invite our friends into our community will they see a group of people which bears the marks of the Holy Spirit's presence?

Ask the group to look at **Acts 2.42-47**. Explain that this is a description of the first Christian community. Ask the group to look at the passage and to identify the evidence of the Holy Spirit's presence among them.

Write the answers on a flip chart so that everyone can see. You should have a list something like this:

- Devotion – to prayer, to the sacraments, to biblical teaching, to fellowship
- Evidence of the supernatural working of God among them
- Lots of praise

- People who were at ease with each other
- Generosity
- Sacrifice
- New Christians joining all the time

Say to the group that some of this we already have in our group and some we don't. Ask the group to tell you what are the things which we do have and what are the things we are yet to experience.

Praying for more

(15 mins)

Now move into a time of prayer. It is best to stand for this.

Begin with praise. Suggest to the group that we praise God for his great plan in sending Jesus into the world and then sending the Holy Spirit into the Church. You are dependent on the ability of the group to compose prayers but encourage them to keep the praise going without long silences, and ask them to keep their prayers brief. Set an example by beginning yourself with a very brief prayer or series of prayers - for example, "Thank you God that your Word is powerful", or "Thank you Jesus that you came into the world", or "Thank you Jesus that you were so full of love".

After a while suggest that it would be good now to begin to thank God for everything he is already doing among you. Again set an example, e.g. "Thank you Lord for the way that I am always welcome here and people are so ready to help me" or "Thank you so much for answering our prayers."

Finally, ask the group to pray earnestly to the Lord for more. This is when you can bring out the things that you wrote on the flip chart earlier.

End this time of prayer by joining hands and standing together in silence. Ask that the presence of God will come upon the group. Leave time for the Holy Spirit to respond and do not be in a hurry to move on.

Bringing our friends into contact with our group   (10 mins)

Tell the group that if we are to reach our 50 friends two things are necessary.

1. We must belong to a community which is filled by the Holy Spirit and so resembles the community in Acts 2.

2. We must find a way of introducing our 50 friends to this community. The Word of God expressed through the community will then do its work.

You should come to the group with the proposal based on the discussion last week for an event to which the 50 friends could be invited. Examples might be:

- I suggest that we book a room at the Swan Hotel and invite our friends for a good meal. After dinner we will listen to a musical item from Fred and then Mary will share the story of her spiritual journey, then I suggest we invite John Jones to be our speaker and ask him to speak on the subject of handling life's difficulties. At the end of the evening we will give those who would like it an opportunity to receive prayer.

OR

- I suggest we organise a family treasure hunt on a Sunday afternoon ending up with a good tea at the church hall. Then we will have a talk from our curate on the subject of 'Real Treasure'.

These are only examples, but you do need to come up with something quite specific. Allow the group to discuss your proposal and make suggestions; promise to come back next week with a final version.

The important things about discussions like this are that

- people should feel that their ideas and their fears are being listened to

- somebody (namely you) will have the courage to make a final decision so that something actually happens.

A time of prayer

End by praying together for the event.

Don't forget to remind them to do the homework during the week.

Beautiful Lives Week 8

Listening to the Holy Spirit

Homework
(15 mins)

Ask each person in the group to share something about the homework as they have experienced it so far in the course. Ask them each to tell one story and each to share one way in which they feel doing the homework has changed them. The time for this is quite short so this exercise should be done in threes.

Jesus and the Woman at the Well
(15 mins)

Ask the group to turn to **John 4.1-26** and ask someone to read the passage. Explain that this is an example of Jesus doing stay evangelism. He did not go to Sychar to preach there – his mission was to Jews, and Samaritan cities like Sychar were outside his remit. He just happened to be travelling through Samaria as a short cut between the south of Israel and the north. On the way, he came face to face with this woman. This is what happens to all of us: as we journey through life, doing our job, raising our families, belonging in our churches, serving our communities, we come face to face with new individuals. Notice from verse 7 that Jesus was exceptionally friendly – the social norm was for a man to never speak to a woman and a Jew never to speak to a Samaritan.

Now look at verses 9-26. Divide the group into threes or fours and ask them to look at the words of Jesus in the passage and ask themselves

48

what was remarkable about them. Allow a few minutes for discussion and a few minutes for feedback.

Observe that Jesus used words which were inhabited by the Holy Spirit and which penetrated to the woman's heart in a remarkably short space of time.

Listening to the Holy Spirit   (25 mins)

Point out that the thing that strikes you most about what Jesus said to the woman is that nothing follows logically from anything else. For example she says "Give me this water" and he says "Go, call your husband". This proved to be just the right thing to say - but how did Jesus know? The explanation must be that while Jesus was listening very carefully to the woman, he must at the same time have been

listening very carefully to the Holy Spirit. What Jesus says throughout this conversation is what the Holy Spirit gave him to say.

Suggest to the group that this insight gives us a new idea. Maybe we could do the same. Maybe the Holy Spirit would help us too to know what to say to people. Say that you would like to assume that he will and try an experiment.

Ask the group to divide into threes or fours and ask one person in each group to be a volunteer. The volunteer should then tell the others how life is going for them at the moment, sharing any particular joys or difficulties. The others are allowed to ask questions but not allowed to give any advice or make any comments at this stage.

After no more than ten minutes interrupt the groups: ask them to stop talking and ask everyone to pray. Tell them that you don't want them to say anything out loud as they pray - you want them to listen to God, just as Jesus must have done as he talked to the woman. Encourage them to ask the Holy Spirit to show them things that were not revealed in the earlier conversation, and then to ask him to show them what to say next.

After at least five minutes of listening prayer interrupt the groups again and then ask those who have been listening to share any insights they have with the original volunteer in their group. If people are unsure whether they are really hearing God, encourage them not to remain silent but rather to say something like "I am not sure but I think God may be saying ...". If anyone has nothing at all they should not be concerned. The ability to hear God like this is found very strongly in some Christians and not at all in others, and the important thing is what is revealed to the group, and not what is revealed to any one individual.

Explain that part of the homework for this week is to try to converse with people like Jesus conversed with the woman at the well. Tell the group that as they talk to people they should listen carefully to them but at the same time listen carefully to God. And if God gives them something to say, they should say it.

Praying for people   (20 mins)

To introduce this section take the group to **Mark 10.46-52** and read it together.

What the Samaritan woman needed was inner healing – her problems were inside, in her heart. Blind Bartimaus was different – we are not told anything about his insides or his moral condition; he had other problems. He had been blind from birth and as a   result had to get his living by begging. The Word of God came to the Samaritan woman through a Spirit-led conversation. The Word of God came to Bartimaus through a miracle. The miracle must also have affected many of the bystanders.

Ask each person present to imagine themselves as Bartimaus. Ask everyone to close their eyes and imagine themselves kneeling before Jesus. Like Bartimaus they cannot see Jesus, but they know that he is there. As people close their eyes you should pray. Thank Jesus for his promise that as two or three gather together in his name he will be there. Thank him that he is here with you now and ask him to speak to each person present.

Say to the group that Jesus is saying to each one of them what he said to Bartimaus: "What do you want me to do for you?" Ask the group to each answer that question – "What do I want Jesus to do for me?" Remind them that Jesus is not asking "What do you want me to do for your wife or your child or your friend" – he is asking "What do you want me to do for you?" Ask everyone to consider – in a few minutes they will have an opportunity to say what it is that they would like to ask Jesus to do for them. If people do not want to share anything then they don't have to.

After a few minutes interrupt and ask people if they would like to share. Do this by going around the room and asking each person in turn. Say that if they have nothing or if they would rather not share just to pass.

When each person has shared or passed say that when Bartimaus put his request to Jesus there was an immediate response. A miracle happened and Bartimaus received his sight. Suggest to the group that perhaps we too will get a response if we put these requests to Jesus right now. For each person who has shared you need someone to pray, so ask for volunteers. For example you might say "John has said that he would like healing for his back. Is there someone here with enough faith to volunteer to pray for John?" and then "Mary has shared that she longs for a husband to share her life. Could someone volunteer to pray for Mary?" Find someone who is willing to pray for each person who has shared and then have a time of prayer.

Explain that the other part of the homework will be to look for opportunities to pray for our non-Christian friends or for people who we meet who have obvious needs. If someone a group member meets has a need which they themselves are in a position to meet, then they should be like the good Samaritan and help that person. But if this is a need they cannot meet, they should offer to pray. They should do this by asking the other person if they have any kind of faith, and if so by suggesting immediate prayer. They should then pray there and then.

Planning an event

(15 mins)

Now is the time to finalise plans for the event to which you will invite your 50 friends. The group will need firm proposals from you which show that you have been listening to their ideas but are capable of making up your mind. The group will need to know the time and place, what the content of the event will be and who the speaker will be.

Give roles to as many in the group as possible, for example preparing food, providing music and so on. Most important of all, hand out 50 printed invitation cards, one for each person to be invited. It is much easier to invite someone to an event if you can give them a card.

End the session with a time of prayer for the event itself and for those who will attend (do not forget to listen to God as well as talk to him), and by thanking God for what has been learned on the course.

In conclusion, remind the group that the greatest expansion of the gospel took place in the second and third centuries. An observation made in the year 150 AD explains why: 'Beauty of life causes strangers to join our ranks. We do not talk about great things; we live them.' It is open to us to do likewise!